THE INTERNAL CONSULTANT
Drawing on Inside Expertise

Marcia Meislin, M.Ed.

A FIFTY-MINUTE™ SERIES BOOK

CRISP PUBLICATIONS, INC.
Menlo Park, California

THE INTERNAL CONSULTANT
Drawing on Inside Expertise

Marcia Meislin, M.Ed.

CREDITS
Managing Editor: **Kathleen Barcos**
Editor: **Follin Armfield**
Typesetting: **ExecuStaff**
Cover Design: **Carol Harris**
Artwork: **Ralph Mapson**

Copyright © 1997 by Crisp Publications, Inc.

Printed in the United States of America by Bawden Printing Company.

Distribution to the U.S. Trade:

National Book Network, Inc.
4720 Boston Way
Lanham, MD 20706
1-800-462-6420

Library of Congress Catalog Card Number 96-87717
Meislin, Marcia
The Internal Consultant
ISBN 1-56052-417-0

This book is printed
on recyclable paper
with soy ink.

LEARNING OBJECTIVES FOR:

THE INTERNAL CONSULTANT

The objectives for *The Internal Consultant* are listed below. They have been developed to guide you, the reader, to the core issues covered in this book.

Objectives

- ☐ 1) **To explain the role of an internal consultant**

- ☐ 2) **To show how to operate as an internal consultant**

- ☐ 3) **To explain closure and implementation**

- ☐ 4) **To discuss dealing with resistance and how to market your services**

Assessing Your Progress

In addition to the Learning Objectives, *The Internal Consultant* includes a unique new **assessment tool*** which can be found at the back of this book. A twenty-five item, multiple choice/true-false questionnaire allows the reader to evaluate his or her comprehension of the subject matter covered. An answer sheet, with a chart matching the questions to the listed objectives, is also provided.

* Assessments should not be used in any selection process.

ABOUT THE AUTHOR

Marcia Meislin, M.Ed., is president of MCM Management Consultants, a company specializing in leadership and change. She has been a consultant for almost two decades inside and outside organizations from diverse industries such as telecommunications, finance, pharmaceuticals, advertising, publishing, and manufacturing.

Marcia earned her M.Ed. at Cambridge College and her B.S. at Cornell University. She graduated from the Gestalt Center of Long Island as a psychotherapist and has uniquely integrated her Gestalt work into the role of organizational interventionist and executive coach. In the evenings, she taught graduate courses at the MBA Program at Pace University, and at the College of New Rochelle. She also designed and delivered classes on "In-House Consulting Skills" at New York University's Continuing Education for Managers Series. Marcia teaches public seminars on consulting, leadership, presentation skills, and team-building.

ABOUT THE SERIES

With over 200 titles in print, the acclaimed Crisp 50-Minute™ series presents self-paced learning at its easiest and best. These comprehensive self-study books for business or personal use are filled with exercises, activities, assessments, and case studies that capture your interest and increase your understanding.

Other Crisp products, based on the 50-Minute books, are available in a variety of learning style formats for both individual and group study, including audio, video, CD-ROM, and computer-based training.

CONTENTS

Introduction vii

SECTION 1   WHAT IS AN INTERNAL CONSULTANT? 1
The Internal Consultant 3
How and Why People Become Internal Consultants 6

SECTION 2   HOW TO DEFINE YOURSELF AS A CONSULTANT 15
What Is the Customer-Supplier Chain? 17
What Do Clients Need from You? 20
Why Consultants Need to Be Real 22
In-house Consultants: Special Considerations 27

SECTION 3   THE EIGHT-PHASE C-O-N-S-U-L-T-S PROCESS 29
The Internal Consulting Process 31
Phase 1: **C**ontact 32
Phase 2: **O**utcomes 38
Phase 3: **N**egotiate Needs 41
Phase 4: **S**earch for Data 46
Phase 5: **U**nderstand and Feed Back Data 54
Phase 6: **L**ay Out Action Plan 63
Phase 7: **T**rack Results 67
Phase 8: **S**et in Motion 70

**SECTION 4   UNDERSTANDING AND WORKING
                        WITH RESISTANCE** 73
What is Resistance? 75
Strategies for Resisting Resistance 78

**SECTION 5   HOW TO MARKET YOURSELF
                        INSIDE THE ORGANIZATION** 81
Positioning Yourself in the Market 83
Describing Your Benefit 87
Packaging Your Services 90
Getting Credibility 92

ASSESSMENT 97

The Internal Consultant

DEDICATION

This book is dedicated to the memory of my beloved parents, Dr. Jack and Millie Meislin. Their love and values are with me all the time.

To my loving husband and dearest friend, Steven Weinstein, and my children, Jonathan and Adam, my life's greatest treasures. They have taught me how to be genuine and real.

To my second set of parents, Sonnie and the late Morty Weinstein and my siblings and their children, Jay, Allan, Donna, Arleen, Mel, Elliot, Eric, Everett, Jared, Bob, Margy, Jordan, Madeline, Richard, Dani, Arleen, Richard, and Shaine. Overwhelming appreciation to all of them.

To my personal and professional friends who reviewed my work in its various stages and gave me honest and constructive feedback and to my favorite consultant, Jamie Telegadis, and most talented colleagues Pam La Sala, Barbara Hahn, T. J. Schweers, Merri Rosenberg, Norma Feldman, and Barry Gold. Malcolm Schryer, from the Bronx Community College of the CUNY, was invaluable for his editing expertise. To Peter Block and Designed Learning, Inc. for teaching me the fundamentals of staff consulting.

Last, but highly coveted, are the terrific internal and external clients with whom I have been fortunate to work. In many instances, my clients, colleagues, and I have been able to establish the kind of relationships in which together we've moved mountains, large and small.

INTRODUCTION

This unique handbook on internal consulting is a collection of principles, exercises, and practices that enable professionals to understand the scope of the internal consulting function while focusing on specific skills for development.

Although this book frequently uses the terms "business" and "corporate," these same principles apply to government, not-for-profit, small business, and volunteer organizations as well.

Through a series of self-paced exercises, worksheets, case studies, examples and self-assessment tools, you can make these theories come to life in your own organizations in a uniquely personal way.

S E C T I O N

1

What Is an Internal Consultant?

THE INTERNAL CONSULTANT

An internal consultant works inside one part of an organization to help another part of that organization. Help usually means solving a problem, enacting a change, giving advice or, in some cases, working on large-scale transformations. What makes the consultant's job unique is that internal consultants work with people over whom they have no direct authority or control.

The difference between internal consultants and external consultants is that internal consultants "live" inside the organization in which they're consulting. They are usually reporting up the line to the same executive management as their clients. Exceptions to this rule might be members of one subsidiary consulting with another subsidiary or merger teams working with an organization that is not yet integrated; but for the most part, "internal" means people working with each other who are within the same system. In this book, we will be referring often to internal consultants—individuals or work teams that support business units that share the same external customer.

Why do people use internal consultants? By definition, a department usually calls in the internal consultant to do one of the following:

✔ Fix or install something

✔ Introduce a new product or service

✔ Solve a problem

✔ Research the feasibility of a certain change

✔ Reengineer, reorganize, relocate, renovate, downsize, outsource, sell, merge, acquire or shut down

✔ Create a new function based on a clear vision and the motivation and support to make it happen

CONSULTANTS' SPECIAL CHALLENGES

Consultants are often seen as "change agents" or sometimes as "change masters." Rarely is a consultant called in to recommend that things stay the same. If that happens, the consultant must stay very tuned into the political climate because he or she might be used as a pawn between the change initiators and change resistors. Few consultants investigate a client's situation and propose that no change be made at that time. Often, just the act of looking at a situation yields one or two opportunities for improvement.

What makes the consultant's job unique is that the consultant has no control over employees' positive or negative reinforcers. When consultants want to make a change or get information or implement recommendations, all they have to fall back on is their own ability to get people to want to join them. This "personal power" as opposed to "position power" can derive from their expertise, their ability to empathize, their prior successes or sometimes from their association with key decision-makers. In some organizations, senior managers give internal consultants certain rights or privileges to bestow as rewards. The irony is that even with these rewards, employees can often make it difficult for consultants to get their job done.

When a consultant is supported by top management but does not have the skills or credibility to create a sense of trust in his or her clients, that consultant is likely to get the runaround by even the least powerful employees in the hierarchy. For example, a consultant may succeed in setting up a new system he or she has recommended. But after a long process of marketing the idea to the employees, training them in the new procedures and providing job aids and operations manuals, a six-month follow-up indicates that no one is actually using the new system!

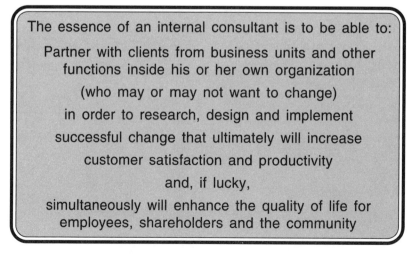

The essence of an internal consultant is to be able to:

Partner with clients from business units and other functions inside his or her own organization

(who may or may not want to change)

in order to research, design and implement

successful change that ultimately will increase

customer satisfaction and productivity

and, if lucky,

simultaneously will enhance the quality of life for employees, shareholders and the community

What Is Your Internal Consulting Experience?

1. How do *you* define the role of an internal consultant?

_____

_____

_____

2. In the capacity of internal consultant, with whom have you worked inside your organization?

_____

_____

_____

3. What types of changes are you called in to help others with?

_____

_____

_____

4. Have you worked on major change in your organization? In what capacity?

_____

_____

_____

5. How would you characterize your ability to influence others?

_____

_____

_____

HOW AND WHY PEOPLE BECOME INTERNAL CONSULTANTS

People become internal consultants two ways—voluntarily or involuntarily.

► **Voluntary:** For various reasons including desire for challenge or greater impact, entrepreneurial spirit or career goals, some professionals choose to consult inside their own companies. Some do it with an eye to becoming an external consultant in the future, and others are happy to have the structure of an organization within which they can carve out more freedom. Professionals who want jobs as consultants will either look for employment in a new organization in that capacity, or they might request a transfer within their existing company to a department that is set up to do that. The more visionary of the group—rarer—create a consulting position where it doesn't exist.

► **Involuntary:** Others have this path foisted upon them because their management has decided their job will change. These people tend to be the less experienced in consulting because their focus was on the technical aspects of the job rather than the consulting aspect. This person may be a human resources generalist, trainer, financial analyst, computer programmer, logistics engineer, technology strategist, product specialist, operations engineer marketer, salesperson or scientist. All of a sudden, the organization decides to transform the person's role from subject matter expert to internal consult.

Consulting Means

You no longer service your client merely as an "information provider," a "subject matter expert," or an "order taker." Rather, you apply your technical expertise directly to a business problem by working at the point of application. Your intervention, meaning the program, project, product or system that you are working on, is a joint effort directly between you and the client in service of the external customer. In consulting, you continually engage in a dialogue about your client's strategic and operational plans, marketing and distribution strategies, how business is changing, what kind of competition is happening in the marketplace and the internal issues that are helping or hindering productivity.

Internal consultants also often participate in task forces, action teams or quality circles from another part of the organization seeking a cross-functional orientation. For those specialists who have always fantasized about making a significant impact on the organization or wanted to get closer to the customer, this is a great way to do that. When staff employees stay inside the organization in "ivory towers," they cannot really see how their work affects the customer. When they visit the business units and the line areas, and meet internal and external customers, they can understand the big picture a lot better and feel a much greater sense of fulfillment.

The other big advantage is professional development. After many years of proficiency in a particular field, people can get stale. In-house consulting experiences can provide invaluable variety, learning opportunities and can prepare people to handle organizational politics and to know what to do with resisters and saboteurs.

If you're going to write your own consulting ticket, you need to explore the kind of compensation packages internal consultants get in your organization. Some places pay a salary, others pay by the contract and others require chargebacks from the internal client. Recent trends indicate that a number of companies have "fee for service" or "chargeback" plans for their internal consultants.

If you propose that you work as though you're in business for yourself inside a larger context, and get paid per project, you have to accept that there might be times of feast or famine. If you present the idea of being compensated through corporate overhead, you will have to prove that your work either increases revenue or decreases costs. In some cases, your results—and the benefit to the company—will not be obvious from the start. Your role in that case, would be to influence the signers of your paycheck that your work has long-term implications and you can justify the investment for the future in a compelling way.

HOW AND WHY PEOPLE BECOME INTERNAL CONSULTANTS (continued)

Career Enrichment

How will learning to be a successful internal consultant be useful in your career? (Check the ones that apply)

☐ Give you a chance to practice your trade in a new way, closer to the customer.

☐ Give you a chance to learn more about the business.

☐ Force you to learn how to market and sell your services.

☐ Provide exposure to more people and more managers around the company.

☐ Give you increased marketability inside your organization.

☐ Show you what it's like to be a consultant.

☐ Help you keep your job.

CASE STUDY: *Lynn Smith*

Lynn Smith was a happy, successful vice-president and training director at a large telecommunications firm. She and her staff were responsible for training all management, professionals and technical staff in the retail sector of the company. But Lynn wondered if the participants who came through her training doors really changed their behaviors afterward. She decided the only way she could really know what was happening on the job would be to get closer to the internal customers, to "live" with them. She created a job description for herself as internal consultant, researching what internal consultants do, how other companies use them, how the job should be positioned organizationally and the kinds of outcomes she would be expected to deliver. When she wrote this all up for her internal customer and boss, they agreed.

The executive Lynn was servicing had several assignments lined up for her. He had come to the organization two years before with the goal of completely transforming the retail sector. What he found was a culture set in the old ways of doing things. He had begun by replacing his senior staff officers with visionary thinkers, but after almost a year, they were stalled in their efforts and the profit and loss statements were not moving in the right direction.

Lynn's job was to spend approximately three months on site with these executives to see what was really going on and to try to "fix" the problems. She was to sit in on their meetings both to understand their end of the business and to assess their communication skills and rapport with their employees. Her other responsibilities included interviewing a cross-section of the employees to get their input and looking at all aspects of human resource development and management techniques. Then she was to give feedback to both levels of management.

CASE STUDY (continued)

The first thing Lynn noticed about her internal consulting job was how unstructured it was. Anything could happen. Moreover, this job was a double-edged sword: To be effective, she had to gain the respect and confidence of the person she was coaching (who did not want her there), but she also had to evaluate if his behavior furthered the new corporate goals. The day-to-day anxiety in this job was high because of the greater exposure to senior management and the need to pass along information that could affect someone's career.

Lynn also gained some perspective on the realities of organizational life. As an internal consultant, she worked much more closely with the business unit as well as with the outside customer and recognized how the tension feels so much greater where the customer transactions were happening. The projects she had worked on, and some of the internal politics and pressure she had dealt with as a staff person were nothing compared to the multi-million-dollar deals that were being put together.

Lynn also knew that her expertise and professionalism were on the line, since a piece of the third-quarter earnings may be affected by her feed-back and recommendations. If she gave a negative picture, the senior executive might choose to replace his division head or to restructure that area. On the other hand, if she painted a positive picture, that same department head would probably continue in her role with an action plan to improve incrementally. Either decision could profoundly affect whether the business moved forward and at what pace. There were plenty of times when Lynn found herself isolated, on the edge, making ethical decisions and substantial business recommendations. However, the work was important, dramatic and exciting, and the personal rewards were long-range. She also realized that these elements were helping make her a well-rounded businesswoman.

> *"The people who get on in this world are the people who get up and look for the circumstances they want, and if they can't find them, make them."*
>
> – George Bernard Shaw

EXERCISE: EVALUATE YOUR CONSULTING COMPETENCIES

Internal consultants often juggle multiple roles and projects. Read each key competency skill category below and give yourself an honest rating from 1 to 5 on each item. This will give you an indication of areas of strength you can capitalize on and areas of development you will need to focus on to become an excellent internal consultant.

Use the following scale to determine your skill level in each area.

1 = None   2 = Needs improvement   3 = Moderate   4 = Good   5 = Excellent/expert

STRONG CUSTOMER-SERVICE ORIENTATION:

____ Respond quickly to customers

____ Spend time learning customer's business and needs

____ Uphold high professional standards

____ Offer alternatives when unable to fulfill requests

____ Educate customers to help them understand processes and move toward greater self-sufficiency

____ *SUBTOTAL*

DIAGNOSTIC SKILLS:

____ Possess technical knowledge in my chosen field

____ Work collaboratively to identify and analyze problems

____ Ask objective questions to make accurate diagnoses regardless of the product or service I offer

____ Make decisions and stand up for my beliefs

____ Use a consulting model/approach to navigate through key phases

____ *SUBTOTAL*

EXERCISE (continued)

ORGANIZATIONAL SKILLS:

_____ Organize work based on goals and priorities

_____ Manage projects within deadlines and on budget

_____ Achieve balance between accomplishing the task and building team support

_____ Lead and participate productively in meetings

_____ Exhibit neatness and accuracy in presenting data

_____ *SUBTOTAL*

COMMUNICATION SKILLS:

_____ Speak articulately and present ideas clearly and with confidence

_____ Listen actively and open-mindedly to others

_____ Read verbal and nonverbal communication signals

_____ Write effective and professional correspondence

_____ Share information and ideas proactively and openly

_____ *SUBTOTAL*

INFLUENCE AND NEGOTIATION SKILLS:

_____ Empower others by collaborating on joint ideas

_____ Exhibit confidence in dealing with all levels of the organization

_____ Negotiate win-win outcomes consistently

_____ Don't take resistance and obstacles personally

_____ Assert my needs with others when appropriate

_____ *SUBTOTAL*

INTERPERSONAL SKILLS:

____ Maintain integrity and authenticity in working with others

____ Build and maintain effective working relationships

____ Handle conflict directly without avoiding or bulldozing

____ Accept criticism without getting defensive

____ Provide supportive, yet constructive feedback

____ *SUBTOTAL*

PROFESSIONAL SKILLS:

____ Market products and services internally in accordance with organizational culture

____ Adapt to change flexibly and practically

____ Continually seek out knowledge and improve upon professional skills

____ Demonstrate commitment, enthusiasm, and energy at work

____ Serve as role model for leadership and positive change

____ *SUBTOTAL*

____ *TOTAL SCORE*

CONSULTING COMPETENCIES FEEDBACK

Now let's take a look at how you did. First look at the score of each skill area to determine if there are specific areas that you need to focus on. Then add up those scores to assess your overall consulting skills and to set objectives for those areas in which you hope to improve.

IF YOU SCORED BETWEEN:

140–175   Consider yourself an accomplished consultant, someone who may even have enough skills to mentor new people entering the field. You're doing well; there may be areas that can be improved even more but you're certainly well on your way.

105–139   You've got a terrific start on the consulting skills. While you may be good at many of the skills now, it appears as though you need more practice and more experience in some of the areas if you want to be considered truly successful. Keep up the good work and use this opportunity to expand your skill base.

70–104   You may have just started in the consulting role and you need more experience and skills in many of the consulting functions. Being an internal consultant is a very tough job and it takes time to master many of the skills listed here. Congratulate yourself on taking the first step and stay open to learning and developing.

35–69   Welcome to the world of consulting! No one said it was going to be easy and there can certainly be tremendous satisfaction in learning new skills and gaining experience. This book will help you through some of the difficult stages and no doubt in three months when you evaluate your skills again, you will see increased results and confidence.

These are the areas of development I have identified to work on first:

_____

_____

_____

I will evaluate these skills again on: _____ (insert date)

S E C T I O N

2

How to Define Yourself as a Consultant

WHAT IS THE CUSTOMER-SUPPLIER CHAIN?

Everyone inside the organization has customers. If your department is in the front line dealing with the company's external customers, you are called a "line area." If you do not have direct contact with outside customers, and your main job is to support the people who do, you are a "staff or support area." Typical staff areas include:

- purchasing
- legal
- human resources
- marketing
- logistics
- technical support
- internal auditing
- research and development
- finance
- accounting
- strategic planning

The main thrust of all of these groups is to *supply* important information or services to the people who directly interact with the company's external, "bread-and-butter" customers—the ones who pay the bills.

Just as every line area has external customers, so every staff area has internal customers, often called "clients or users." Inside customers have to be treated with the same sense of urgency and responsiveness as do outside customers. If they don't get the quality service they need in a timely fashion from their suppliers and service providers, then they can't treat the "bread-and-butter" customers right. And the company will lose business.

> "If you're not serving the customer, your job is to serve someone who is."
>
> —Karl Albrecht and Ron Zemke,
> *Service America*

Customer-Supplier Chain

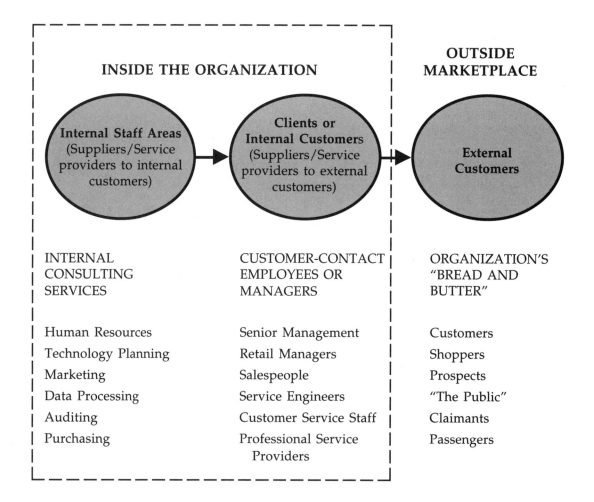

INSIDE THE ORGANIZATION

OUTSIDE MARKETPLACE

Internal Staff Areas
(Suppliers/Service providers to internal customers)

Clients or Internal Customers
(Suppliers/Service providers to external customers)

External Customers

INTERNAL CONSULTING SERVICES	CUSTOMER-CONTACT EMPLOYEES OR MANAGERS	ORGANIZATION'S "BREAD AND BUTTER"
Human Resources	Senior Management	Customers
Technology Planning	Retail Managers	Shoppers
Marketing	Salespeople	Prospects
Data Processing	Service Engineers	"The Public"
Auditing	Customer Service Staff	Claimants
Purchasing	Professional Service Providers	Passengers

HOW DO YOU FIT INTO THAT CHAIN?

Using the previous page as a model, see if you can fill in who your customers and suppliers are. In the circles, write the names of departments or groups that you interact with in the capacity described. On the lines below the circles, indicate individual customers or suppliers with whom you have the most significant contact. This diagram will help you recognize how you fit into the customer-supplier chain.

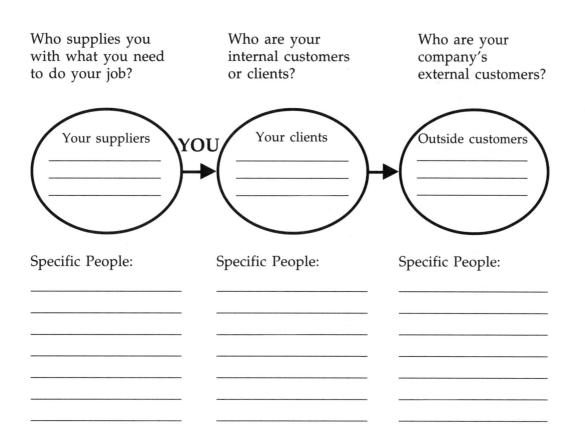

Who supplies you with what you need to do your job?

Who are your internal customers or clients?

Who are your company's external customers?

Your suppliers

YOU

Your clients

Outside customers

Specific People:

Specific People:

Specific People:

WHAT DO CLIENTS NEED FROM YOU?

To be customer focused, the best starting place is to understand your customer's goals, strategies, requirements and concerns. Pick one of your significant internal customers from the previous diagram. The following questions will help you collect enough data to answer the question, "What do my clients need from me?" If you already know the answers, you might sit down with your internal clients and verify your point of view, just to make sure you are in sync with their business needs.

Some of your assignments may be to work with other staff areas. Remember that they expect the same quality, quantity and speed of work that line personnel expect, because their internal customers have high demands of them, as well.

The words "client" and "internal customer" are used interchangeably, as are the terms, "customer" and "external customer."

Client's name: _____

1. Client's department or business unit: _____

2. Who is your client's customer (your internal customer's customer)?

    _____

    _____

3. What type of product or service does your client provide?

    _____

    _____

4. What is your internal customer's long-term mission or strategic direction? Marketing and distribution strategies?

    _____

    _____

5. Over the next one to two years, what will be your client's greatest marketplace challenge?

_____

_____

6. What kind of help will your client need in order to face this challenge?

_____

_____

7. How can you or your department help your client reach short- and long-term business goals?

_____

_____

8. How can you give your internal customer more than standard help? What sort of "value-added" benefit do you offer above and beyond your role?

_____

_____

9. If you're already working with this person, how does he or she rate you in customer responsiveness and satisfaction? What feedback has he or she given you?

_____

_____

10. What important points do you need to keep in mind for future work with this client?

_____

_____

WHY CONSULTANTS NEED TO BE REAL

Executives lead a paradoxical life. They want to know what's going on in the organization but they don't have access to the "real people" who will tell them the truth about what is happening. Over the last few decades the consultant has filled a critical need in organizations as a listening board and a provider of honest and objective feedback.

John Geirland and Marci Maniker-Leiter wrote, "Five Lessons for Internal OD Consultants." In that article, they state the importance of honesty in the client relationship, especially for internal consultants.

> "The internal consultant's candor in expressing organizational realities is what the job is all about; that candor is the added value that he or she brings to the organization. . . . The most important and challenging of the five lessons [for internal consultants] is to show courage. You probably will be called on to say things to your clients that they would never hear from their peers or subordinates—or even from the people they report to." From, *The 1996 Annual: Volume 2 Consulting*, edited by J. William Pfeiffer

CASE STUDY:
"I Want to Hear the Truth. No, I Don't."

ABC Corporation decided to conduct a comprehensive written study of how employees in the organization felt about working there. They hired an expensive, prestigious outside consulting firm to design and administer the survey to all employees.

The results indicated that management practices and the overall climate were not conducive to employee satisfaction. Upon hearing the news, the CEO dismissed the survey, claiming that the consulting company was not credible and had erred in administering the instrument. Therefore, he said, the results were invalid.

Employees had been promised a meeting to review the survey, but meetings were not held until a full eight months after they had answered the questions. The CEO thanked them for filling out the survey. He then told them the data they would be hearing was not valid because of major problems with the administration of the instrument. He concluded that management agreed there were a few minor adjustments to make, but overall the company was truly an excellent place to work, and he was sure that everyone concurred with that view.

Why do you think the CEO and management rejected the survey?

_____

_____

_____

_____

WHY CONSULTANTS NEED TO BE REAL
(continued)

Author's Response

As an internal consultant at the time—though only an observer and not directly involved—I learned four memorable lessons:

Lesson 1: Most People Are Ambivalent about Hearing Honest Feedback

The people at the top of an organization are no exception. They ask for feedback; they beg people to be straight with them. Sometimes, however, the responses don't match their notion of the truth, and they react in various ways. Here are some unfortunate reactions:

- They stay in denial and pretend there was no survey.

- They take it personally and get defensive.

- They get angry and take it out on the people who responded or the consultants who conducted the survey.

- They find a different scapegoat.

- They pat themselves on the back for the fact that their people feel safe enough to be open and honest with them in a survey.

- They set up committees (and subcommittees) to investigate the findings.

- They accept everything at face value, get overwhelmed and do nothing.

Lesson 2: They Often "Shoot the Messenger"

It is not uncommon for a consultant to be the purveyor of bad news and the one who gets "shot" in the process. A good consultant requires a lot of courage because it isn't easy to come forward and tell people things they might not want to hear, particularly people in powerful positions. It's especially dicey when you are one of their employees and you have a vested interest in staying on the payroll. That's one of the reasons why politically volatile or sensitive projects such as effectiveness surveys or expense-cutting task forces are often led by outside vendors in conjunction with inside departments.

We always run the risk of not being appreciated for our candor. The problem is that many of us feel guilty or troubled if we believe we had that precious information and *didn't* share it with someone to better the organization. It takes guts and a passion for making things right to be a good consultant. Tact is important, so you know how to say things that don't upset or offend people. More on that later.

Lesson 3: Build Rapport and Trust with Your Client Before Beginning Intensive Work

Entering delicate territory with your clients tends to work a lot better when they already know you, respect you and believe you are doing what you do for the right reasons. When clients start second-guessing your motives ("Was she sent here by someone to fire me or to spy on me?"), you lose your credibility and they don't trust you. The only way clients will take important risks with you is if they feel somewhat secure in your presence based on a prior relationship of trust, credibility and support.

Some consultants are so eager to be armchair psychologists that they plunge right in to a person's private life before they are invited to do so. I have also been in situations where I thought we both felt comfortable, so I launched into my "diplomatic confronting mode," only to find that the other person resented me because he felt we hadn't gotten to the point in our relationship where I could be so invasive (even if I knew how to do so "nicely").

WHY CONSULTANTS NEED TO BE REAL (continued)

> **Lesson 4:** Client Resistance Can Happen Anywhere, Anytime and at Any Level

Resistance can occur at any stage of a project or a relationship, even if everything up until then seemed fine. If a person feels threatened or uncomfortable in some way and doesn't know how to tell you that directly, she throws up a smokescreen and the process comes to a screeching halt. Particularly if she's the officer-in-charge (OIC)!

Imagine if the OIC had been able to call in the consultants and say, "Look, I'm uncomfortable with these results. They're very negative and they imply that my management team and I are not running the organization well. That upsets me. It makes me feel threatened. It makes me angry. It makes me think twice about my future here. But my salary is so big. How will I find another great job like this one? I'm scared and I need help sorting this out. Can you help me?"

This isn't resistance. This is an open, healthy dialogue about how to use the feedback wisely and how to see this as a peak learning experience. The consultants would feel empathy for the OIC and the atmosphere would enable honest sharing and problem solving to take place.

* More often, people find it hard to identify or talk about their feelings. Then the resistance gets muddy and confusing, decent projects are tossed and the executives remain isolated. Consultants need to learn the cues so they can catch potential problems *as* they arise, not in the eleventh hour. They need to have excellent observation skills, keen insights into people and a bold, daring ability to ask provocative questions about what is going on and why.

---

* The scenario above, though refreshing, is an unusual occurrence.

CONSIDER THE FOLLOWING . . .

IN-HOUSE CONSULTANTS: SPECIAL CONSIDERATIONS

Some in-house consultants feel that it's harder to be a change agent when they *"live where they work."* There is a lot of pressure when you're making the transition from "whatever you were" to internal consultant. You were perceived one way by your constituents and now you are asking them to believe you have these problem-solving and political skills. You may have evolved from a caterpillar into a butterfly, but if you have done this within one organization, there will always be people who swear you must still be that caterpillar who sat in the office next door for two years.

Another stress is staying power. External consultants can come into a company, wreak havoc, and then decide not to work there again. They're off to other contracts in other places. Some talented internals may have this option as well, but most have to come back day after day even if things didn't go well in a previous contract. They have to be even more resilient and know how to handle delicate situations and recoup from their losses. Internals don't have the luxury of walking away from a place, so they need to develop confrontation techniques to use as needed, assertiveness skills and a thick skin to overcome early traumas.

Whether your job is to recommend new computer equipment, to get a cardiac drug to market before the competition, to cut staff by 20 percent or to conduct internal audits, your greatest asset as a consultant is your integrity and your ability to be "real." This means bringing your whole self to the situation so you can be there to listen fully when people confide in you about their jobs or their equipment or their fears. At any given moment, you might need to be a friend, a coach, an information-provider, a messenger, a devil's advocate, a human being, an interpreter, a partner, a whistle-blower or an extra set of hands. If you stay flexible to the needs of the organization and true to who you are, your value as a consultant will definitely grow.

The Client-Consultant Relationship

A Delicate Balance

"BEING YOURSELF"

SUPPORTING	**CHALLENGING**
Hand holding	Being objective eyes
Empowering others	Empowering self/others
Respecting client resistance	Confronting resistance
Reacting/"Putting out fires"	Proacting/Preventing fires
Being a friend	Playing Devil's Advocate
Getting deeply involved	Keeping clear boundaries

SECTION

3

The Eight-Phase C-O-N-S-U-L-T-S Process

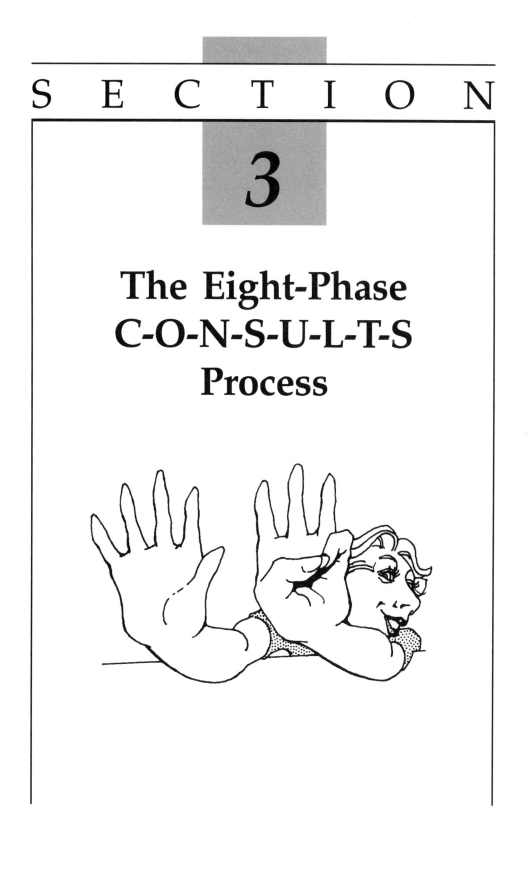

THE INTERNAL CONSULTING PROCESS

The consulting process can sometimes seem unwieldy so it's useful to break it down into easy-to-remember steps. If you remember the word CONSULTS, you can remind yourself how to be a consultant. Using this acronym, we have detailed many of the specific skills that go into each phase of the consulting process.

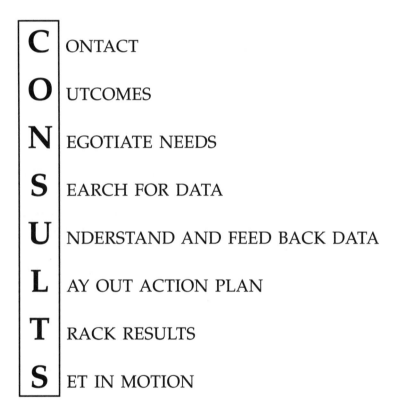

C ONTACT

O UTCOMES

N EGOTIATE NEEDS

S EARCH FOR DATA

U NDERSTAND AND FEED BACK DATA

L AY OUT ACTION PLAN

T RACK RESULTS

S ET IN MOTION

PHASE 1: CONTACT

Important points to remember about the contact phase:

✔ Client or consultant identifies need for change and contacts others for a meeting.

✔ Learn as much as you can about the client, his business unit, and his marketplace before first meeting.

✔ Leave problems, fears, biases, and insecurities outside the door.

✔ Make a genuine connection with the client; practice eye contact, listening skills and empathy.

✔ Pay attention to your observations, perceptions and gut reactions.

✔ Be clear in your mind about who the client is.

✔ Don't try to bypass parts of the process; take things step-by-step.

Contact begins when the initial communication is made. The term, "moment of truth," typically used to describe customer service encounters, refers to any opportunity in which a customer is likely to form an impression of you or the department you represent. Often, when a client has a moment of truth (or vice versa) about you early on in your relationship, he is formulating a more generalized opinion about what working with you will be like. For example, if the client calls your office and the phone is answered by a temporary worker who doesn't know where you are, the client may already be making some negative assumptions about how you operate. But if you send a potential client an article you read in a professional publication that has relevance to her operation and you attach some ideas relative to her business, the client may begin to perceive you as proactive and helpful.

What different ways can contact be made?

- Initial call comes from the client looking for help.

- You call client because you see an opportunity to help.

- Your boss sends you on the assignment.

- The client's boss invites you in to work with them.

- A third party, such as a consultant from another department, brings you in.

First Impressions

Our first moments of truth in the eyes of the customer or the prospect may be positive or negative. If it's a first positive moment of truth, then you have begun contact on a good note. These moments of truth may be something you feel you have no control over, such as one day when your voice mail isn't working and you don't get the message and the client calls back irate one week later. On the other hand, the entire way you handle that initial problem can open the door for a lot more positive perceptions.

By the time the actual face-to-face meeting occurs, the client already may be holding a tacit "moment-of-truth report card" that shapes his decision to go with you or not. Can I trust this person or not? Trust may seem like an intangible. Yet, when we analyze what makes up trust, it is probably a combination of gut feel and a lot of mini behaviors from the past and the present. These moments of truth work the other way as well; they are openings for consultants to decide if they're comfortable with the client.

PHASE 1: CONTACT (continued)

Contact, then, is a lot more than a simple phone call or get-together. The feelings that each party brings to the event early on can affect the way the partnership evolves. In the initial meeting, the consultant's main job is to listen. If the client has initiated the call, she obviously has something on her mind. While the consultant must come prepared with a list of potential questions, the real reason for the questions is to get the client to open up. If you have a client who is more than ready to tell you everything that's going on, your job is not to interfere and to use that time to get a real sense of the individual and the challenges he is facing. Only in this way can you see whether you can work successfully as partners. This decision has as much to do with believing in each other (Will I feel okay about this person "meddling in my affairs"?) as it does with your technical ability to do the job.

The best way to have real contact in this phase is to be yourself. When clients reveal their problems to someone, they need to know that the someone will respect their confidentiality and their vulnerability. The characteristics we are talking about are integrity and ethics.

In that first dialogue, try to get the big picture. You'll want to know what that unit's goals are, who its customers are, what it's already done to deal with this issue, and how effective those steps were.

FINDING DECISION MAKERS

It is important to know who the key players will be. Find out the following:

- Who is the key client?
- Who is the target group?
- Who has the power to make "go/no go" decisions?
- Who needs to be involved in the process?
- Who has the most to gain or lose from success or failure of the intervention?

Generally two or more levels above the target group within the vertical chain of command is where you will find the person with authority. It is quite common for a consultant to spend a lot of time with the person who called her in, only to find that person has no power to make decisions. Some decision-makers want the consultant to meet with a lower-level employee who can do the screening and discuss the preliminaries of the logistics. However, veteran consultants can tell hundreds of stories regarding their conscientious efforts to satisfy their clients based on those preliminary meetings, only to find that the person paying the bill completely disagrees with where the project is headed. Then, when it's time to explain why the project went off track, this lower-level employee who was sent to meet the consultant and coordinate the project disappears or disavows any knowledge of the project. The consultant can end up the scapegoat.

The beneficiary of the intervention is usually called the "target group." It is just as important to set a good tone with the target group as it is with the key client. If good rapport is established early with the people for whom the intervention is intended, then the consultant has a better chance of succeeding. While it is true that an executive endorsement does make for safer passage, a better guarantee of victory would be working both top-down and bottom-up. With the backing of a president, CEO or any key person in power, the rank and file probably would not resist the change openly. Yet we all know how changes can be sabotaged in private and through the grapevine. Therefore, when a consultant is fortunate to have top management's endorsement, he should not take for granted that the client or the target group will agree. Most programs should be tackled on a multilevel approach to ensure the longevity and full acceptance of the change.

> **NOTE:** Some companies send consultants out in teams. If you are part of a team, you need to meet with the other members before visiting the client. In this preliminary meeting, you will want to discuss who does what and how you would like to interact with each other in the client's presence. Stay in **contact** with your fellow consultants as you would your client.

WHEN IS THE BEST TIME TO MAKE CONTACT?

Usually, top managers in an organization do strategic planning for their area and, based on this long-term plan, they develop specific shorter-term action plans. When employees start implementing the action plans, problems often surface. If not dealt with, they can become crises. Consultants are generally brought in at that point to "put out the fires."

If you can establish good enough rapport with your client to be brought in at the strategic planning phase, your contribution can be far greater than if you're brought in to do "damage control" or "disaster recovery."

How can you ensure that your clients use your services "proactively," not just "reactively?"

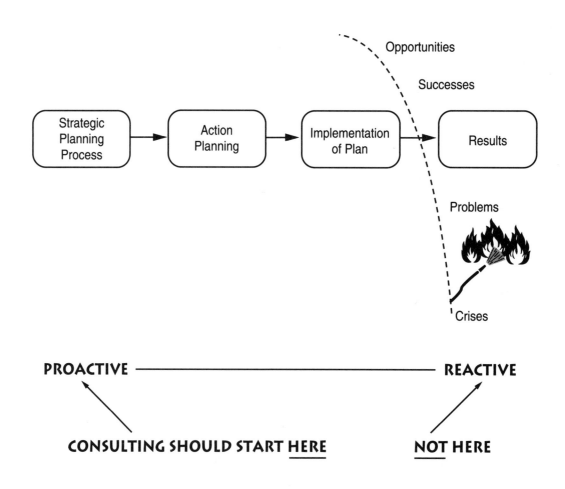

CONTACT OBSERVATIONS

Understanding your client's style and personality is as important as understanding his or her goals. Here are some questions to keep in the back of your mind when you're meeting with someone on a new project. It's not necessary to do anything with your answers; simply be aware of your initial impressions.

- ► Has this person put distractions away, indicating a willingness to focus?

- ► What kind of nonverbal communication is this person exhibiting; what does her facial expression and body language tell you?

- ► When you two are talking, does she make eye contact or does she look away? Is the pace of her voice hurried or slow? Does her body language reflect that she is in a hurry or that she seems to be taking her time?

- ► What does this person's environment reveal about what's important to him? Pictures of family all over? Piles of reports or academic journals? Plaques or trophies on the wall?

- ► How open is the person to questions or to challenges? Does he expect you to take things at face value or does he encourage you to say what's on your mind honestly and openly?

- ► How willing is this person to work with you? Is she there under coercion (because her boss wants her to meet with you) or does she earnestly want your help on a problem?

- ► How much "pain" does this person seem to be in regarding the problem? Does it appear as though you're talking about something that can be fixed with a Band-Aid or something that will require major surgery? How quickly do you need to move on this project?

PHASE 2: $\boxed{\text{O}}$UTCOMES

Important points to remember about the outcomes phase:

✔ Encourage the client to articulate desired outcomes from the intervention.

✔ Help the client use word pictures, metaphors, symbols and examples to gain clarity.

✔ Ask yourself how you feel about that outcome; is this something you will feel comfortable supporting?

✔ Ask the client to describe how the outcome will be viewed from all related areas.

Once the client can communicate a picture of what he'd like that outcome to be, it's much easier for the client-consultant team to work together without constantly referring to the box to see what the final picture looks like. Unless you know where you're headed, you'll be faced with a constant struggle working piece by piece.

Guideline Questions

A. Imagine that you are able to create the exact situation or environment that you envision. Describe exactly what this optimal state of affairs would look like. (Another way to ask this: Imagine that you are flying in a helicopter above your organization and everything is going exactly the way you want it to. What would you be seeing, hearing or feeling?

_____

_____

_____

_____

_____

_____

B. How is this different than what's happening now? (If you were flying over your organization right now, what would you be seeing?)

_____

_____

_____

C. If you make this change, what other parts of the organization will be affected? How?

_____

_____

_____

D. Who else needs to be involved in decision-making for this project? How will they participate?

_____

_____

_____

Questions to a client involve not only where he or she is headed. Ask, What's supposed to happen when you get there? "What effect will this change have on the people you want to affect?" "What will it feel like, look like, sound like, to your customers?" It is helpful for the client to articulate this outcome using metaphors, symbols, images and graphics, as well as words and examples. If the outcome can be described in a multisensory form of communication, through visual, auditory, and kinesthetic modes, this too, will captivate more listeners.

The more clarity you can achieve in this phase, the better.

CONSULTANT'S ANALYSIS OF THE SITUATION

At this point, you want to take inventory of where you are and ask yourself certain questions to make sure you're on track.

Who exactly is my key client?

_____

_____

_____

What do I know about my client's strengths, weaknesses, motivations, concerns, preferred mode of communication, best time of day?

_____

_____

_____

What does my client stand to gain or lose from this change?

_____

_____

_____

Who is my target group for this change? What do I know in a preliminary fashion about the group's current situation (strengths, weaknesses, opportunities, threats), its mission, purpose, history and political climate?

_____

_____

_____

PHASE 3: NEGOTIATE NEEDS

Important points to remember about the negotiate needs phase:

✔ Clarify expectations, needs and wants.

✔ Negotiate a formal or informal contract.

✔ Make preliminary decisions about who will do what and when.

✔ If you are experiencing any signs of resistance or conflict, consider raising the issue.

✔ Summarize all previous agreements and understandings.

✔ Send a letter of agreement, contract or proposal as agreed.

This early negotiation that goes on in the relationship can affect much of what comes later. In this phase, the client and consultant *both* have a chance to express their needs for the project. The process usually begins with the client. The client might:

- need you to finish the job in six months.

- need you to work with his or her department full-time until the merger is complete.

- need to work through his or her assistant.

- ask that you be completely honest with him or her throughout your work together.

COMMON NEGOTIATING POINTS

These and dozens of other possibilities could arise in the negotiation phase. Below are the main elements that usually get covered in this phase and some common examples of a consultant's negotiating point.

Time Commitment on Both Sides

"I understand you want this job completed in six months. My take on the job is that it will take more like eight months because of the equipment we are working with. If you want it in six, I'll need one person on your staff to work with me full-time for about a month to analyze the data."

Method for Data Gathering

"In order to succeed at the product you've asked me to develop, I will need to spend some time talking to your customers, conducting focus groups and perhaps doing a quick phone survey to see what they need. In my experience, these three methods combined will yield the most accurate information for our purposes. What are your thoughts about this combination of research methods?"

Specific Objectives and Timeframes

"We've agreed on the methodology for collecting data. If we can complete the engineering study by the end of March, we can have a draft of the design by July. Pending all the approvals, construction can begin around August or September. Is this the schedule you had in mind?"

Administrative Support

"As we agreed, you will provide the clerical support to type, copy and send out the information for Tuesday's meeting. My responsibility is to make the overheads and confirm the equipment. Is that how you understood our discussion?"

Budget

"As I'm sure you are aware, our department charges back for the training programs that we run for the business units. Our costs are $xxx per day. This project will require four days of design time and three days to deliver the program. That would mean $xxx plus materials and expenses. Those fees would have to be paid by the end of first quarter. Is that agreeable to you?"

Check-in Periods

"In order for me to best serve your needs, I need to meet with you to discuss the status of the report at least once every two weeks. Because the deadline is so tight, if we don't meet, we run the risk of going off course. The product would then take twice as long."

Ongoing Form of Communication

"What is your preferred method of communication?" . . . "In the past, a lot of my clients liked me to e-mail them on important developments, and then when we met face-to-face, we got into the people issues."

Relationship Issues

"I hope that you'll be very honest with me as we go through this project. I'm very open to feedback and I'd rather that you tell *me* if there is a problem, than tell my boss or anyone else before I get a chance to resolve it. I hate to feel that problems may be festering and I can't do anything about them."

Location/Office Space

"I'll probably need to spend about three days a week here going through the records from the last strategic plan. Is there an office I can use or a vacant conference room with a telephone that I can work in on those days?"

COMMON NEGOTIATING POINTS
(continued)

These examples reflect a customer-oriented consultant who wants to achieve his client's objectives. Professionals new to the field, however, may find some of these statements too assertive at the beginning. Some people coming from a staff position aren't used to bargaining for what they need; they're used to filling requirements as order takers or being called in as experts to solve a small piece of the puzzle. In this case, where the consultant will be managing a whole project or investigation, she needs to make the path clear for everything to go right. If that means asking for people, equipment, supplies or money to get the job done, then ask! The worst that will happen is the client will say no, and if that impedes the project in any way, then a discussion will ensue. Eventually, if the client is committed enough to the outcome, a mutually satisfying solution will be found.

A new consultant often becomes concerned when his key client delegates the liaison work to a subordinate and tells the consultant that she doesn't need to work with him anymore. In some instances that works out fine, but in many situations he will need to be aggressive about maintaining some form of communication with the initial client, even if it is sporadic.

If your client expects something of you that you can't fulfill, you should state that up front and give the reason why. It's better to know what issues might come up now than to find later that there is a big misunderstanding. Being honest and real will make this partnership work.

When you are all done with your negotiating needs, the consultant writes out what he and the client agreed upon. In the letter of agreement, contract or proposal, all of the items listed above are spelled out so there's no disparity later regarding the terms of the project. Even when the client and consultant are the best of friends, a simple memo restating what was said is advisable. The contract also should be fluid enough to renegotiate later if changes occur.

Additional Points to Clarify

1. What do you expect from a consultant? What type of help are you looking for from me? (What are your needs and wants in this relationship?)

_____

_____

_____

2. How do you feel (or, What are your thoughts?) about what we've said so far?

_____

_____

_____

3. Who are the formal and informal leaders in this part of the organization? Whose "buy-in" will I need in order to implement an action plan?

_____

_____

_____

4. When can we review the desired outcomes, agreements and next steps for this project?

_____

_____

_____

PHASE 4: $\boxed{\text{S}}$EARCH FOR DATA

Important points to remember about the search for data phase:

✓ Decide on the best method for gathering data.

✓ Research the business' culture before interviewing.

✓ Conduct interviews, surveys and site visits.

✓ Pay attention to the task as well as to the relationship issues.

✓ Compile data in a readable and clear way.

Data gathering takes many forms. The one you choose will vary depending on the nature of the project, the organizational culture, budget and time constraints, the size of the population to poll, and your personal preference. The most popular data collection techniques include:

- Informational interviewing
- Surveys

- Focus groups
- Direct observation

- Flowcharting
- Analysis of existing records

- Literature review
- Videotaping

- Benchmarking (measuring against best industry practices)

- 360° feedback (polling a client's customers, colleagues, boss, and subordinates, and an objective person provides feedback to client regarding the circle of perceptions.)

Regardless of which you choose, the great challenge is in picking the right cross-section of people or papers to investigate. Try to step back from your research group and see if you really are getting an objective picture. If, for instance, you want to explore how a new benefits program will be received by the employee population, don't just ask the people in your department or at your location. If you're in headquarters, the field offices may have quite different reactions to the plan, and vice versa. It is not uncommon to hear a corporate staff department saying after the fact, "I don't understand why this new program didn't catch on. I polled everyone who was in the executive dining room for a week straight!"

Generally, consultants end up using several methods of data gathering to get the most accurate diagnosis.

WHY DO DATA GATHERING?

Why spend a lot of time on data gathering? Why not get going right away toward the solution? By the time you finish doing all those surveys or asking all those questions, the problem could have long been solved. This query is a valid one. In fact, some places do so much gathering that they suffer from "analysis paralysis." Other places like to spend their time wrapping the data into immaculate reports. By the time these graphically perfect reports are organized into decks for the next board meeting, the economy has changed and the figures are no longer relevant.

Yet, there is a fundamentally important reason for conducting the "search for data" phase. The people steeped inside the situation can rarely evaluate all aspects of the issue from where they sit. The outsider who comes in with ostensibly little bias (or at least less than the people who live there) is not locked into the same assumptions. At the beginning, you notice everything because your eyes are sharply peeled to pick up everything of interest. After awhile, you start focusing on what you're doing and these things fade into the background, and eventually become almost invisible. That's why a new set of eyes can usually do a better job of assessing what's going on than an insider who "lives in the neighborhood."

The most compelling reason that this blind spot happens over time is because people "can only focus on" what's going on in the moment, and can't see past that. It's especially true if there are big problems, and all the client can think about is, "Get someone in here to fix this problem before we all drown."

Consulting pioneer and teacher, Ron Lippitt, in *The Dynamics of Planned Change,* summed it up very well in his statement, "If the system is currently in pain or trouble, that in itself may generate defensive obstacles to accurate self-diagnosis. The pain may be so great that attention is riveted upon symptoms: the client's only clear thought is that the symptoms must be removed."

WHY DO DATA GATHERING? (continued)

THE DOCTOR! DOCTOR! STORY

Imagine what would happen if a patient came into the doctor and said, "My side hurts so much. Give me an appendectomy." The doctor says, "Okay," and removes the patient's appendix without asking any questions or taking any tests. Lo and behold, the patient comes back the next week and says, "Doc, I'm still in pain. What did you do? You didn't cure my problem. It must be a kidney stone. You gotta take it out. I need surgery!" Again, the doctor says, "Okay." Well, that isn't it either. The doctor does just what the patient wants each time but doesn't get it right because she is taking the patient's word at face value without using her own expertise as a diagnostician. True, this process is a partnership: the patient knows how he feels and what his body tells him but the doctor knows what questions to ask, what tests to take and what data to search out before treating the patient. Not only can misdiagnoses aggravate a condition further, but they waste precious time and dollars, they make the patient angry, they don't address the root of the problem, and they can lead to expensive malpractice suits!

► Do most of your clients tell you their symptoms for a joint diagnosis or do they try to diagnose the problem themselves?

_____

► Can you think of a time your client's self-diagnosis was not accurate?

_____

► Why did this happen?

_____

Questions to Ask in Your Search for Data

These questions are sample questions that can be used in the data-gathering phase.

1. Who are your customers?

2. What product or service does your unit provide?

3. How are you structured to provide this service?

4. How effective is your unit in satisfying your customer's expectations? What works and what doesn't?

5. Describe your contribution to the problem.

6. How do others contribute to this problem?

7. What has already been tried to remedy the situation? What was the outcome?

8. What process do you follow in handling this transaction?

9. What are the best parts of this process? Do they always work well?

10. Which parts of this process continually get off track? Why?

11. What kinds of formal and informal communication go on between your internal customers and suppliers?

12. How confident are you of reaching this goal? Why?

13. What is the possibility of your group failing to reach this goal? Then what will happen?

14. What resources are available to help you achieve your aim?

15. If you were a consultant coming in to this business unit, what recommendations would you make to management on how to fix the problems for the long-term?

16. In thinking of your desired state, which of these areas represent the greatest gap between where you are now and where you want to be?

INFORMATIONAL INTERVIEWING GUIDELINES

One of the most common and effective forms of data collection is the interview, which gives the consultant both objective and subjective information. Having both viewpoints is helpful if there's a chance that what you propose will meet with resistance. In the interview, you can ask questions and read the person's reactions through body language, tone of voice, and facial expressions. The secondary benefit is to elicit buy-in or ownership from the people you interview. If a change is introduced using ideas generated in the personal interview or if you reflect the person's language in communicating the idea, she feels more a part of the result. When this occurs, people are more likely to embrace the new reform.

The down side of this method is that it takes longer than some other techniques. It is harder to interview a large number of people. The alternative is to send out a written questionnaire and conduct an informational interview with a smaller cross-section of the group.

Interview Guidelines

There is a good chance you will be using a face-to-face, phone, or satellite interview with your client and the immediate people involved in the decision making for the intervention. Therefore, we have included key points to remember in setting up and carrying out the interview.

Setting Up the Interview

- Schedule ahead of time

- State the purpose

- Let the interviewee know what records to gather

- Try to schedule on his territory to make him feel more comfortable

- Ask permission to tape record, if needed

Preparing for the Interview

- Find out about the person you're interviewing

- Determine your objectives

- Write out prepared questions

- Familiarize yourself with the environment, culture, industry and the client's business

Starting the Interview

- Arrive a few minutes early

- Start the interview in a friendly manner to make the interviewee comfortable (small talk only if appropriate)

- Restate the purpose of the meeting

- Discuss confidentiality

Conducting the Interview

- Let the interviewee do most of the talking

- Start with open-ended questions (requires more than yes or no answer)

- Move into closed-ended questions as you need more specific information

- *Listen* to what's said—and not said; probe but be sensitive to resistance

- Refrain from using leading questions or inquisition style of questioning

- Maintain a relaxed style, smile and use the person's name

- Find a diplomatic way to keep interviewees on track if they diverge

- Stay away from vague abstractions and avoid using jargon

INFORMATIONAL INTERVIEWING GUIDELINES (continued)

Listen Actively

- Look at the interviewee

- Sit up; don't slouch

- Keep an open mind; let the person finish without making a judgment

- Give supportive, nonverbal clues ("um hum")

- Restate what the person has said to ensure you understand it

- Handle the resistance (see chapter on resistance)

Taking Notes

- Ask permission

- Look at the interviewee as often as possible

- Write down key words, good quotes, statistics and facts, questions to pursue later

- Look for main ideas and themes

Closing the Interview

- Thank the interviewee

- If the interview is not going well, stop and ask what's happening

- If the person is totally adversarial or unhelpful, end quickly

- Suggest the interviewee call you if she thinks of anything else

- Discuss next steps

- Write up notes or transcribe tapes as soon as possible

PHASE 5: UNDERSTAND AND FEED BACK DATA

Important points to remember about the understand and feed back data phase:

✔ Organize information into format to present to the client.

✔ Provide feedback of your findings to the client.

✔ Get the client's ideas and recommendations.

✔ Use "pull" as well as "push" techniques—influence rather than authority.

✔ Spend a lot of time listening without judgement.

✔ Balance feedback; good news as well as not-so-good news

Now that the data is organized for discussion, you need to sharpen your skills on giving feedback. The most effective feedback is balanced; you give some good news and some not-so-good news, but you always tell the truth. The consultant needs excellent skills in formulating the feedback so that it is heard and received by the client. The biggest difficulty consultants have is learning how to talk about the more sensitive aspects of their research, because they are afraid they might hurt someone or the client might get angry at hearing it. What they forget is that it's only through feedback and communication that a company can achieve its highest goals. Your challenge as a consultant is to recognize that honest feedback is a gift that brings tremendous opportunity for attaining peak performance.

THE THREE METHODS

> **Method 1: Gap Analysis**
>
> **Method 2: Force Field Analysis**
>
> **Method 3: The Four Ps**

Method 1: Gap Analysis

Gap analysis looks at the difference between peoples' or business units' optimal and actual performances and determines what is needed to bridge that gap. Begin with a clear picture of the client's vision and what result she would like to achieve if everything were working perfectly. Then examine the reality of what's going on right now in the organization. This way, you get a full picture of the discrepancy between where you are and where you want to be.

Once you have illustrated the current situation and the vision, you can take actions and make choices to bridge the gap between here and there. This discrepancy forms the basis of the unified plan to bridge the gap between the current situation and the desired results. The following graphic shows how to apply the model.

DESIRED RESULTS
(OPTIMAL STATE)

PERFORMANCE GAP

Actions needed to get from actual state to desired state

CURRENT SITUATION
(ACTUAL STATE)

THE THREE METHODS (continued)

Method 2: Forced-Field Analysis

If a heavy object is sitting in one place, and an attempt to move it doesn't succeed, it is easy to think that the forces around the object are lazy or lacking in energy. That's not the case. The reason that the object doesn't move is because there are equally strong pressures on it at the same time to hold it back. Because these opposing forces exert more or less the same amount of power, nothing will happen. The object will not yield.

Similarly, in organizational behavior, the tendency is to view status quo organizations as being inert and static. That's hardly the case in a dynamic system such as an organization. Kurt Lewin, a noted psychologist, observed that at any given moment forces will be trying to change the organization or an aspect of it and other forces trying just as hard to keep it in balance. The only ways to make the change, then, are either to increase the forces driving the change, add new driving forces, decrease or eliminate the forces hindering the change, or a combination of all of them.

Remember the other law of nature: for every action, there is an equal or opposite reaction. What makes change difficult is that organisms and organizations strive to stay in balance. An example of this is when a new process is introduced into an organization; it's not surprising that people develop selective memories and can only remember how perfect the old system was. When using the force-field model as a diagnostic tool to pick the right treatment plan, all of these natural forces to maintain equilibrium should be considered.

After gathering the facts, the data can be formulated in the form of a force-field analysis to study the level of force that is helping the unit move toward its goal and the level of force moving it away from the goal. Indicate these drives on a diagram by drawing arrows toward or away from the change, with each arrow representing one of the forces in operation. Draw a long arrow for strong forces and shorter arrows for less forceful dynamics. After plotting all of the forces onto the diagram, it's easier to see what appropriate actions should be taken.

FORCE-FIELD ANALYSIS

The following force-field model can be used to analyze a problem you are dealing with.

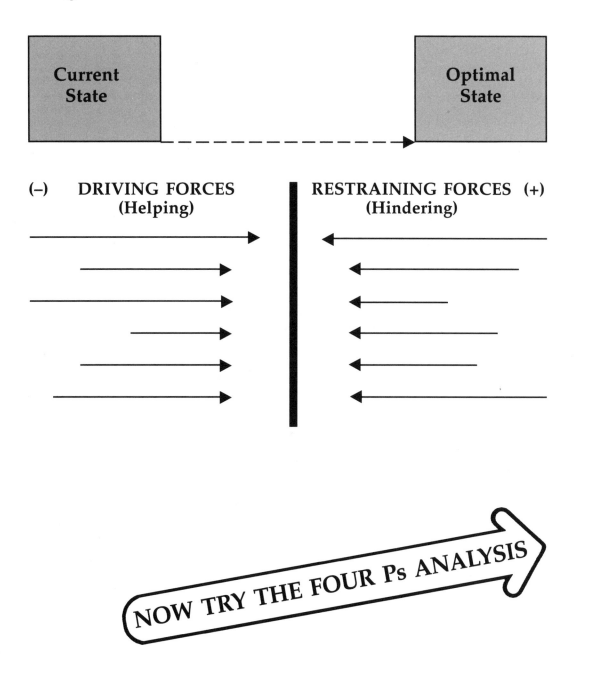

THE THREE METHODS (continued)

Method 3: The Four Ps Analysis

This method is essentially one more way you can look at the volume of data that you gathered in Phase 4 of the CONSULTS process.

One way of collating data, though old-fashioned, is to work with a letter- or legal-sized writing pad. Pull out eight pages. On each page, write a heading:

- Purpose—Strengths

- Purpose—Areas of Improvement

- People—Strengths

- People—Areas of Improvement

- Product—Strengths

- Product—Areas of Improvement

- Process—Strengths

- Process—Areas of Improvement

As you go through all your data, add the relevant information to the appropriate page. You can write it out or cut and paste. Continue this process until all the data is in its appropriate place. You also can do this work directly onto a computer.

As you transfer the information to a computer or elsewhere, you can reorganize the data in each section any way that will work best for your client. Your four diagnostic categories should cover the key elements of any task. You may need to have a page labeled "Miscellaneous" for any additional comments.

Questions to Ask Using the Four Ps

Purpose

- ► Do all the departments understand the goal?

- ► Are they all working toward the same goal?

People

- ► How well do the people function as teams?

- ► Is leadership strong?

- ► Are managers managing performance and holding their people accountable?

- ► How well do employees communicate with each other?

- ► How is conflict handled?

Product

- ► What is the quality of the product or service that is being offered?

- ► How well does the product fill a niche in the marketplace?

- ► What are the defect rates? Return rates?

- ► What is the level of customer satisfaction or dissatisfaction with the product?

Process

- ► How effective is the internal process from manufacturing through delivery?

- ► What policies and procedures, structures and operations exist to get the product or service out the door to content customers?

- ► How effective is technology?

- ► Is the physical environment set up to best achieve the objectives?

- ► Is work flow organized correctly?

THE THREE METHODS (continued)

Key Questions About Data Analysis

1. What thoughts do you have as you read the three methods of outlining data that are demonstrated?

_____

_____

_____

2. Can you see how different approaches may be used in different situations?

_____

_____

_____

3. Do you have a personal preference?

_____

_____

_____

4. Are there any other forms of analysis you like to use?

_____

_____

_____

TIPS FOR RECEIVING FEEDBACK

► Let the client know up front that your feedback will be balanced. The sandwich approach starts with the positives, moves into the areas for improvement, then ends again on a positive. There are some people who don't like this technique because they are always waiting for the "other shoe to drop."

For the average individual, however, it seems to work best, even if the third part of the sandwich is omitted.

► Give the person time to respond between comments. Make every effort to read his expressions to see how he's doing so you can adjust your tone accordingly.

► You don't need to apologize or make excuses for telling the truth. Your job was to gather the information and report it as you heard it, saw it and analyzed it.

► Try to relate the facts without being judgmental or editorializing too much.

► Give examples to clarify your point. Anecdotes, observations and unattributed quotes all help make your point.

► Be specific. Avoid generalities.

► Ask for "feedback on the feedback" to ensure that your message is being received correctly.

► If you're given positive feedback, don't disclaim it. Just say "thank you."

► When you're given negative feedback, don't get defensive. Thank the person for the feedback and go home and think about it. Consider feedback a gift!

PREPARATION FOR THE FEEDBACK MEETING

As a checks and balances system, ask yourself if you have covered all the bases:

☐ I have separated fact from inference and opinion.

☐ I have packaged my data so that the client hears all the information—both good and not so good.

☐ My motives are "pure"—to help a business unit achieve its goals rather than to enhance my career or political standing.

☐ I have the strength of my convictions to stand up for my work even if the client wants to dismiss it.

☐ I am well prepared. I have covered all of my bases and done all my homework.

PHASE 6: $\boxed{\text{L}}$AY OUT ACTION PLAN

Important points to remember about the lay out action plan phase:

✓ Keep ongoing communications with all involved.

✓ Stay tuned to internal or external conditions that can affect the plan.

✓ Consistently monitor commitments of formal and informal leaders.

✓ Meet deadlines and manage checkpoints.

✓ Jointly plan appropriate actions, including how to get commitment at all levels. Clarify roles for the implementation phase.

✓ Plan how to make the transition from where you are to where you want to be.

✓ Set up contingency plans.

Now that you have reported the data to your client, you will be developing a mutually acceptable plan. You will be laying out the key actions and responsibilities. Part of the plan will be how the transition phase will be organized.

DEVELOPING A UNIFIED PLAN

After you have presented the data to the client in whichever format you choose, you need to develop a mutually agreeable plan for addressing the issues. Since most issues have complex causes and consequences, pick the most critical concern. If it's a problem situation, zero in on the one issue that, if corrected, would have the most impact. If you are involved in a start-up operation, pick the main aspect that would lead most closely into the vision.

Then suggest that you and the client discuss strategies for tackling that main issue.

Activity #1

You can begin with a brainstorming technique in which you and the client come up with as many ideas as you can think of without judging them or commenting on their merits. This technique is even better if you bring more people into the discussion. After you have written down as many ideas as you can, you go back over the list and pick the strategies that will work best. The advantage of this method is that it generates a lot of ideas in a short period of time and people "piggyback" off each other's thoughts. The downside is that some people may not be comfortable asserting themselves in this environment, so you as facilitator will need to ask them specifically for their thoughts.

Activity #2

Try the "Round Robin" activity. If you have more than two people in the room, you write the stated problem on a flip chart. Then you go around the room and each person offers one idea on how to fix the problem. You keep going around the room until people have run out of ideas. The advantage of this technique is that everyone gets a chance to speak.

DEVELOPING A UNIFIED PLAN (continued)

Activity #3

A third method is to break the problem up into subcomponents or sub-problems. Each person writes one of the subproblems on top of a piece of paper. He or she writes one suggestion on how to solve the problem. Then each passes the papers to the person on her left, who writes another solution. All the papers get passed around until everyone has commented on each aspect. The papers are reviewed for the ideas that will yield the best solution. This method is better for people who think more clearly on paper than out loud.

WHAT OTHER IDEA-GENERATING SOLUTIONS DO YOU USE?

_____

_____

_____

_____

_____

_____

_____

_____

WRITING OUT THE UNIFIED ACTION PLAN

Now that you and your client have selected an intervention, you need to design a project plan that is thorough and clear. You don't want anyone to say later that they didn't know they were responsible for something. You don't want any aspects of a plan to slip through the cracks. In your plan, be sure to include these action steps:

1. What needs to be done and in what order?

2. How is it to be done?

3. Who is to do it? How will they be told? Who is the backup on each step of the plan?

4. Where and when will each step be done?

5. What contingency plans will you set up in case you have a problem?

6. How will you know when you have achieved success? (What specific measures will you use to evaluate?)

7. What role does the client need to play in the implementation phase?

8. What role does the consultant need to play in the implementation phase?

9. How often will you check in with each other?

10. How are you going to get buy in from:

    - Senior management?

    - Your internal and external customers?

    - Your co-workers?

    - Your staff?

    - The transition team?

    - Anyone else?

PHASE 7: $\boxed{\text{T}}$RACK RESULTS

Important points to remember about the track results phase:

✓ Set up mechanisms to measure successes and problems.

✓ Be open to receiving constructive feedback.

✓ Celebrate interim successes.

✓ Conduct "lessons learned" meetings for projects that fail.

✓ Test out intervention in a small area before implementing fully.

✓ Offer ongoing support and resources.

✓ Keep doors open for future business.

You have arrived at an important part of your journey! The first thing to do is to test out your idea in one area, often known as a pilot. Then, measure the outcome to assess if the quantitative and qualitative results were achieved. If they were, you are at the pinnacle of your process, and it's time to create a ritual to mark the success. If it's a positive outcome, have a party or an event thanking all involved for their efforts. A nice, meaningful way of saying "we appreciate you" as soon as possible after the completion, even of the pilot, is a big reinforcer. These programs need not be expensive.

Different people are motivated by different things. Some appreciate a letter of commendation from their boss thanking them for their efforts above and beyond the average workload. Some appreciate being sent to a desired training program; others relish greater visibility with senior management. Many appreciate time off, though to others it means they'll have even more work to catch up on when they get back. One unique form of gratitude was when a transition team leader wrote a letter to a spouse of one of the employees who had worked very hard on the team. In addition to the note thanking the spouse for putting up with the hardship and long hours of the project, the team leader sent a certificate of appreciation, and two free theater tickets to compensate for the time they didn't have as a couple in recent months.

After the commemoration is over, finish documenting how the consulting intervention took place up to this point. You may want to use a checklist format to help you replicate the process in the future. Do it while the information and the steps you took are fresh in your mind. Then ask others who were technically involved in the project to add their comments to the work so you have a thorough road map for next time.

PHASE 7: TRACK RESULTS (continued)

If the project didn't achieve the outcomes that were set, sit down with your client for a "Lessons Learned" meeting. Avoid finger-pointing and placing blame. An interesting strategy comes out of negotiating techniques in which both you and the client sit on the same side of the table. Sitting side-by-side rather than on opposite sides allows you to tackle the problem as collaborators rather than as adversaries, which is sometimes the tendency when programs don't go as planned. As always, start the discussion by finding at least one positive outcome first. Keep the tone of the meeting developmental and curious rather than evaluative and judgmental.

Questions to Consider

The last thing is to reflect on how well you did as a consultant. You can start with a self-evaluation and then ask your client to give you feedback. How you conduct yourself in the final stage of the process may be as important as the moments of truth you exhibited throughout the project.

▶ Did the plan work as measured against the outcomes?

▶ What follow-up methods do you plan to use to make sure these new changes are accepted and institutionalized?

▶ How can the unit celebrate even small successes to keep up morale?

▶ How can you document what went on so you can use it to learn from and to plan future events?

▶ What feedback can you and the client give each other that will be helpful for the future?

▶ Ask the client, "Will you use me again?"

▶ Ask the client, "How else can I help you?"

SELF-EVALUATION AFTER EACH PROJECT

1. What did I do well on this project?

_____

_____

2. What could I have done better?

_____

_____

3. How would my client evaluate me on this project?

_____

_____

_____

4. If I were my client, would I work with me again?

_____

_____

5. If I didn't do well, what is my plan for "damage control?"

_____

_____

6. How can I put closure on this project so that my client will want to work with me again in the future?

_____

_____

PHASE 8: $\boxed{S}$ET IN MOTION

There is a growing trend today for internal consultants to be called upon actually to participate in the implementation of their recommendations. If your plan is extremely well written and thought out and if it has been communicated to all affected parties, this part of the process will not be terribly difficult. A good consultant has played out all aspects of the transition in his or her head and has worked out major problems in advance. Sometimes, however, things will go wrong. To some extent, this can be counteracted through a few proactive strategies:

1. Set up communication channels where a nondefensive, easy dialogue can occur as soon as a problem is spotted. The goal is to have a minimum of time elapse from the time the difficulty is identified to the arrival of a team sent out to neutralize the problem.

2. Sometimes resistance to the change will be covert. In those instances, architects of the change have to practice active listening skills in a way they've never practiced before. They need to be able to pick up signals of resistance, underground mumblings or plans to sabotage.

3. Contingency plans are never to be locked up in a safe for very long. The actual plan and its backups should be reviewed periodically through the change process to stay clear about all the ramifications.

4. If somebody is transferred, resigns or in some way cannot continue her role in the transition, the person assigned as the alternate or backup should move in immediately. If that person cannot assume the leadership throughout, he can serve in an "acting" capacity in the interim so that the target population always knows to whom to go.

5. "Management by walking around" is as important as ever. By wandering around as the intervention is happening, you might notice if anything was inadvertently omitted from the plan or if unexpected issues are surfacing.

Questions to Consider

► Be aware of any natural resistances that may surface here such as, "We don't have time, money, staff or equipment," or, "We tried that already and it didn't work." Try to identify the resistance and point it out to the client in a way that is supportive yet direct. What resistances do you see coming up now?

► Revisit your project plans or action steps to clarify or renegotiate:

1. Who is responsible for what? (Primary and alternate)

2. What action plans need to be taken?

3. When are these steps due?

4. Where will each step take place?

5. How will the plan be communicated, managed and implemented?

6. Why is this happening? What is the measure of success?

► What contingency plans will you set up in case you have a problem?

► What role do you need to play in the implementation process?

► How can you market the plan so you get all constituents to buy in?

► What special accommodations are you going to make to cover the double-duty shift of the transition phase and the regular customer requirements?

S E C T I O N

4

Understanding and Working with Resistance

WHAT IS RESISTANCE?

By definition, resistance means "the act of resisting, opposing, withstanding . . . a force that retards, hinders or opposes motion." No wonder there is so much concern in the consulting world about resisters! If enough people band together to oppose the motion of change, then it is hard to incorporate a new invention or idea into an organization. Conventional wisdom has it that resisters are to be squelched, put down or managed out so that the organization can get on with the job of making change.

What the corporate world often doesn't realize is that this reaction has as much to do with the method of introducing change as the change itself. Sometimes the people who initially are the most vocal against the change turn into the strongest proponents of the change later on. Much of that has to do with how they were brought into the process, how well they were listened to and how much input they had along the way. Michael Hammer and James Champy, in *Reengineering the Corporation,* state that in a reengineering process, "A leader doesn't coerce people into change that they resist. A leader articulates a vision and persuades people that they want to become part of it, so that they willingly, even enthusiastically, accept the distress that accompanies its realization."

This book has repeatedly addressed the importance of communicating with all levels of the organization from the time a change is conceptualized to the time it is institutionalized. Emphasis has been placed on getting "buy in" from the lowest to the highest levels of the company. Hand in hand with this concept has been the philosophy of being a consultant who is genuine and real, who doesn't lie to people or cover things up. A good consultant maintains integrity and trust with her clients and the target group she is affecting.

Communication and integrity help diffuse the intensity of the resistance because people feel free to express their concerns throughout the process. If consultants are sensitive to certain fundamentals of human behavior and they are not terrified of people who disagree with them, they can plan an intervention that invites resisters into the process so they feel empowered and respected.

WHAT IS RESISTANCE? (continued)

Check those actions you plan to use

☐ I will explain the reasons for the change.

☐ I will talk to people in person.

☐ I will tell people the truth.

☐ I will solicit questions and find answers if I don't know.

☐ I will give people the opportunity to express their feelings.

HANDLING RESISTANCE

Resistance is not the same as admitting openly that you're uncomfortable or unhappy with something. Resistance is when you are uncomfortable or unhappy and you can't say it outright so you try to camouflage the feeling and it comes out anyway. You are hiding your feelings behind a smoke-screen of saying that everything is fine when it really isn't. In the world of work, especially, we are trained not to speak openly but rather to pretend everything is okay when it isn't.

The best thing to do in these instances of personal resistance is to stop and ask the person what is happening. The question, "why are you acting like that," though common, is not terribly helpful. Most respondents say, "I don't know," or, "acting like what?" A more effective approach would be to tell the person what you observed. "In that last comment you made, it sounded like you were angry. Are you angry with me about something?" With a client, you might say, "Brook, when we met the first time, you seemed so enthusiastic about the new product we were developing. The last few times we had a meeting, either you haven't shown up or you've been extremely quiet. Is there a problem we need to address either with the product or with me?"

After you say what you need to say, remain quiet and give the other person a chance to respond. If you express a genuinely caring manner, hopefully, he will feel safe enough to tell you what's really going on. Then you can get all of the issues out on the table and have a dialogue about how to resolve the problems. If he doesn't choose to share his feelings at that moment, the best you can do is to let him know that you are truly concerned and whenever he is ready to talk, you will be interested in listening. If that approach doesn't encourage him to open up, it will probably get his problem closer to the surface.

STRATEGIES FOR RESISTING RESISTANCE

The following principles are helpful if you want to promote change and collaborate with those who have different ideas about what they'd like to see in the workplace.

- Resistance is not only a normal part of the change process, but it can be a healthy reaction.

- Resistance is not a personal attack against the consultant.

- Your listening skills are the best tool you have.

- Stick with your principles but compromise on smaller issues.

- Make sure the decision-making executive is communicating frequently with the staff.

Your Own Blocks

Think of times in your own life when you weren't comfortable with a change and you wanted to block it but you had trouble facing it directly.

What are some of the ways you typically hide your feelings?

_____

_____

What sensations do you experience in your body that let you know something is not quite right?

_____

_____

What strategies can you use to listen more closely to your body or your intuition when it's trying to tell your brain something important?

_____

_____

APPLYING WHAT YOU LEARNED

Here's a chance to see how much you have learned about consulting. Think of a consulting job that you might be called in to do. If you have had a recent consulting assignment, refer to that project as you answer these questions.

How do you rate yourself on your ability to balance task and relationship issues?

_____

_____

_____

Think about the seven phases of the internal consulting process. How well do you handle each phase? Which parts come easily for you? Less easily?

_____

_____

_____

How authentic are you in relationship with clients? How can you be more "real" with your clients?

_____

_____

_____

What forms of resistance do you see in the organization?

_____

_____

_____

APPLYING WHAT YOU LEARNED
(continued)

What verbal or nonverbal clues do you observe that let you know there might be resistance?

_____

_____

_____

How do you plan to handle the resistance?

_____

_____

_____

Based on what you learned through this book, what would you do differently if this or a similar project came up in the future?

_____

_____

_____

What are the two or three skills you want to work on most? What resources do you have to help you develop in these areas?

_____

_____

_____

How to Market
Yourself Inside
the Organization

POSITIONING YOURSELF IN THE MARKET

If you think of the consulting business as a crowded open-air market, your "stall," or niche should stand out from the crowd in a distinctive way. According to Al Ries and Jack Trout, positioning "gurus," the easiest way to get into a person's mind is to be first—the first one to provide this type of product or service. For many of us, it would be a hard sell since the "first" spot (the one closest to the door?) is usually taken. What else draws attention? What else would make a customer decide to browse *and* purchase at your stall when competitors are all around?

In many cases, you won't have an opportunity to market yourself because your clients and your niches will be predetermined by your bosses. However, this skill of figuring out your niche in the marketplace if you were to have a more open stab at the market will certainly help you in your future.

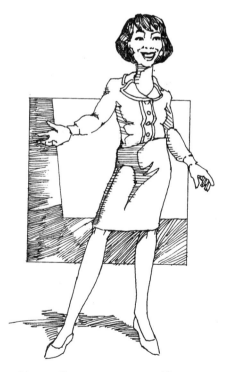

How will you set yourself apart from the competition?

Why Me?

The following survey will get you thinking about creating your special place in the customer's mind. After contemplating all of these angles, and answering the questions below something might jump out at you that answers the question, "Why you?"

1. Who are you? (Ten words or less)

   _____

   _____

2. What are you selling? (What are your skills and benefits?)

   _____

   _____

3. What is unique about you?

   _____

   _____

4. Who would want to "buy" your services?

   _____

   _____

5. Why? (What benefit would a client get from engaging your services?)

   _____

   _____

6. Who might not be interested in what you have to offer?

   _____

   _____

7. Why not?

_____

_____

8. What could a client expect from you?

_____

_____

9. What internal or external consultant or other provider is your biggest competitor?

_____

_____

10. What do you offer that your competition can't?

_____

_____

11. What are some of your drawbacks?

_____

_____

12. How do you compensate for these drawbacks?

_____

_____

13. What does your "packaging" say about you? (i.e., attire, image, marketing materials, your correspondence, your office)

_____

_____

WHY ME? (continued)

14. To what extent does your "packaging" reflect what you want it to say?

_____

_____

15. How would you describe your market niche? Where do you think your services will have the biggest appeal?

_____

_____

16. What is your strategy for targeting your market?

_____

_____

Create Your Positioning Statement

Summarizing what you said on the previous pages, write a short statement, or an executive summary, on how you would position yourself in your potential customer's mind. Think in terms of what they need that you are uniquely qualified to provide. Identify who your target market is and one or two strategies you will employ to capture that market.

DESCRIBING YOUR BENEFIT

Imagine that you heard about a division of your organization within your domain that could desperately use your help, but the members don't know it yet. The manager in charge is new to the organization, so you've never met her and even your boss can't make the introduction. You are about to make a "cold call."

Milo Frank wrote a book called, *How to Get Your Point Across in Thirty Seconds or Less.* His research indicates that the attention span of the average individual is about *thirty* seconds! Let's assume that you have thirty seconds to grab the manager's attention to set up a face-to-face appointment so you can talk directly to her about her needs. To make it easier, pretend you get her voice mail when you call, so you don't have to worry about her responses.

Marcia Meislin's Sample 30-Second Message
(The parentheses represent the number of words)

Hello, Mr. Crisp? My name is Marcia Meislin, and I own a management consulting firm in New York (18). I noticed in your catalogue that you have excellent business books on all sorts of topics but there's not one single book for internal consultants (43). Since this is such a hot topic now, I thought you'd want to read my manuscript on how to be an internal consultant (66). It's interactive, like all your CRISP books, it's practical, and I know it will knock your socks off. (84) How about if I send you a prospectus, and some sample pages? (96) My number is: 914-ABC-DEFG. (100)

NOW IT'S YOUR TURN. READY? GO . . .

Thirty seconds equates roughly to 100 words. Write down in 100 words or less who you are, why you are calling, and what benefit the other person will get from meeting you. It's helpful to use a hook, something snappy at the beginning of the call, to arouse interest.

Start in pencil with a good eraser. The parentheses next to certain lines indicate the number of words you have written.

_____ _____ _____ _____ _____
_____ _____ _____ _____ _____ (10)
_____ _____ _____ _____ _____
_____ _____ _____ _____ _____ (20)
_____ _____ _____ _____ _____
_____ _____ _____ _____ _____ (30)
_____ _____ _____ _____ _____
_____ _____ _____ _____ _____ (40)
_____ _____ _____ _____ _____
_____ _____ _____ _____ _____ (50)
_____ _____ _____ _____ _____
_____ _____ _____ _____ _____ (60)
_____ _____ _____ _____ _____
_____ _____ _____ _____ _____ (70)
_____ _____ _____ _____ _____
_____ _____ _____ _____ _____ (80)
_____ _____ _____ _____ _____
_____ _____ _____ _____ _____ (90)
_____ _____ _____ _____ _____
_____ _____ _____ _____ _____ (100)

NICE JOB!
THAT WAS TOUGH!

After you compose your basic message, take a stopwatch or a timer. Practice saying these sentences and see how long it takes. Are you over or under thirty seconds?

Listen to yourself as you say the words; then ask:

- ☑ Do I make sense?

- ☑ Am I credible?

- ☑ Does my passion for my topic come through?

- ☑ Am I genuine so I don't sound like a bad infomercial?

- ☑ Do my words feel right for me?

If the answers to any of these questions are "no," then go back and change your thirty-second message. Perhaps you haven't found the right combination of words to describe what you do. Perhaps you're lacking the confidence to assert yourself. Maybe you're not used to calling someone you don't know and introducing yourself with conviction. Maybe you're uncomfortable talking to voice mail. Keep working on your message until you feel good about who you are and what you are presenting.

PACKAGING YOUR SERVICES

In today's streamlined world, the topic of marketing consulting services internally is a very sticky one. Spending time figuring out a marketing strategy and then developing marketing materials seems out of place in lean organizations where every dollar spent had better be earmarked for the customer or as close to the customer as possible. Somehow the notion of sending around slick brochures or designing fancy and expensive web sites displaying your wares is anachronistic in an environment where the company might have just frozen salaries, announced a decline in quarterly earnings or laid off part of a workforce.

Clearly the best way to develop and retain internal customers is to demonstrate expertise in your field, establish strong relationships, continually update your knowledge and enhance leadership abilities. If you're in an organization where you are assigned to a particular client group, they know what you can do for them and you have plenty of repeat and new business, then you don't need to send out any promotional materials. You will still want to ensure that all of your memos and materials are professional and recognizable, but you won't need to spend time or money on your "visual identity."

Circumstances that lend themselves to the development of internal marketing materials include the following:

- The consulting department is a start-up operation.

- Internal consultant's client groups are not aware of its capabilities.

- Internal customers are in remote locations.

- Competing service providers hand out literature.

- Your information has to get out to a large organization.

- The services provided changed or expanded.

- You are in an organization where this is the norm for staff departments.

- Your products serve a special need or circumstance or they have seasonal value.

- Your function is outsourced.

Learning how to present yourself and your department visually is something that can be simple, inexpensive, and fast. Computer-literate employees using easy software packages often can produce a basic home page or capabilities brochure in a short period of time. The first thing to do is to talk with your manager. If your department hasn't traditionally created marketing materials for distribution, find out why. Some companies have taboos about it. Still other groups want to sell their services but don't know how.

A growing population of internal consulting groups are on a fee-for-service plan, and they are able to act more autonomously as a business. Rather than reduce consulting staffs, some companies reduce the pay for their salaried consultants and encourage them to work both inside and outside. In these instances, formal marketing is very important. Senior consultants whom I know have negotiated with their companies to have a certain number of days off to do paid consulting work on the outside. If your function has been outsourced, you need to sell to more than just your own company.

Look around at materials sent by other consultants or consulting companies. What do their materials say about them? Is their logo a symbol of what they do, or is it their initials, or some other mark of distinction? Is the tag line next to their brand name indicative of their function, or their positioning in the marketplace? What instant picture do you get when you hear the tag lines, "Tom's; The Natural Toothpaste," or, "Avis; We Try Harder"?

If your organization fosters entrepreneurialism, it's doubtful that you will have a problem allocating resources to design and marketing. Usually, the biggest stumbling blocks are time (professional consultants would rather be consulting than designing marketing materials or selling themselves) and self-doubt ("I don't know how to put myself on paper"). It's not an easy process but it feels good when it's over. You can look proudly at your stationery and matching envelopes, your video demonstration tape, your industry newsletter, the half-page article in the company newsletter, the nameplate you have hanging in your office describing what you do, or the logo that accompanies everything that goes out of your office. All of these elements contribute to your total packaging and hundreds of positive moments of truth a day.

GETTING CREDIBILITY

Credibility is defined as your believableness. How do you get people to trust you and believe in you as a consultant? The following checklist offers some suggestions on how to become credible and valued inside your own company. As you read each suggestion, put a checkmark in the boxes that indicate practices you already do well. When you finish reviewing the whole list, place an asterisk(*) next to those items in which you want to improve. Your commitment will be even stronger if you include a future date for checking your progress in the development areas you picked.

I. STAY IN TOUCH WITH WHAT'S HAPPENING IN YOUR COMPANY AT LARGE

☐ Keep a strong network of contacts inside the organization.

☐ Read and collect the company's literature and articles in the media.

☐ Ask your boss and colleagues to keep you posted on changes in the organization, even in departments that you don't interact with regularly.

II. KNOW YOUR INSIDE AND OUTSIDE CUSTOMERS

☐ Learn about your client's business and about its customers.

☐ Ask customers if you can visit them onsite to see firsthand what they do.

☐ Go on (external) customer visits with your line client.

☐ Learn your customer's language. Make it your business to understand the jargon so you don't feel like an outsider.

☐ Research your customer's position in the marketplace. Know where it stands relative to the competition, and what it needs to do to gain more share of market.

☐ Build strong relationships.

III. FIND OUT WHAT HURTS THE MOST OR NEEDS ATTENTION

☐ Listen to the areas of greatest pain. Evaluate whether they are bleeding slowly or hemorrhaging. If they're hemorrhaging, deal with the crisis but don't lose sight of the underlying causes to focus on later.

☐ Study your customer's strengths and weaknesses. Listen to what she tells you is happening, but make your own independent observations as well.

☐ Give honest and constructive feedback on what you observe.

☐ Practice "CBWA" ("Consulting By Wandering Around"), meet the employees. Listen! Listen! Listen!

☐ Learn to read verbal and nonverbal cues, especially when there is resistance to change.

IV. DEVELOP AUTHENTIC CLIENT-CONSULTANT RELATIONSHIPS

☐ Respect the sacredness of confidentiality agreements.

☐ Make sure your own "baggage" isn't interfering with the relationship or the outcome.

☐ Show flexibility in being able to move from a supporting stance to a confronting one if needed or anywhere in between.

☐ Stay alert to social and political "hot buttons."

☐ Don't gossip or get involved in the "rumor mill"; certainly, don't start rumors.

☐ Manage your "moments of truth"—every detail that comes out of your office can create a perception in your customer's mind about the operation as a whole.

☐ Be known around the organization as a person with integrity and ethics.

☐ Learn to say "no" in a way that people end up thanking you for saying it.

GETTING CREDIBILITY (continued)

V. CREATE PRODUCTS AND SERVICES THAT ARE PRAGMATIC YET INNOVATIVE

☐ Don't try to be "all things to all people"; find your niche and be the best at what you've chosen.

☐ "Think globally but act locally"—respond to your customer's immediate needs for "putting out fires" but work simultaneously with an eye on the big picture.

☐ Keep in communication with your clients. For them, you may be "out of sight, out of mind." While their work may be your top priority, you may be lower down on their priority list.

☐ Give as much consideration to how you're going to communicate and gain acceptance for an intervention as you do for the intervention itself.

☐ Don't be afraid of pizzazz. Even the most senior managers become bored by humdrum recommendations.

VI. MARKET AND SELL YOUR PRODUCTS AND SERVICES INTERNALLY

☐ Break into the market where you know you can have a successful pilot. Then get your satisfied clients to give testimonials of your work to others.

☐ Involve senior management in your implementation strategy. If they really like it enough, they'll end up marketing it as their idea, which, in most cases, is good for you.

☐ If your customer repeatedly rejects what you have to offer, find out why. Either adjust your product to their specifications, create a new marketing strategy, or cut your losses and get out. If the timing is right at a later date, pull it out, repackage, and try again.

VII. PERSONAL STYLE

☐ Don't take criticism personally; people will stop telling you the truth and you'll never learn from your mistakes.

☐ Do not be the type of person who needs positive ego stroking all the time.

☐ GET A LIFE outside of your job, too! In order to stay balanced and not overinvest yourself to the point where you lose your objectivity, involve yourself in nonconsulting interests. If you keep your eggs in several baskets, you will also have a lot more fun in your job because you will know how to keep your work and your life in perspective!

Assessment

THE INTERNAL CONSULTANT

THE INTERNAL CONSULTANT
DRAWING ON INSIDE EXPERTISE

A FIFTY-MINUTE™ BOOK

The objectives of this book are:

1. to explain the role of an internal consultant.

2. to show how to operate as an internal consultant.

3. to explain closure and implementation.

4. to discuss dealing with resistance and how to market your services.

OBJECTIVE ASSESSMENT FOR THE INTERNAL CONSULTANT

Select the best response.

1. An internal consultant
   A. has no control over those advised.
   B. works only within one organizational site.
   C. may advise many organizational sites.
   D. A and C.

2. An internal consultant's ability to make change happen is based on
   A. personal power.
   B. positional power.

3. Internal consultants are mainly
   A. problem solvers.
   B. information providers.

4. Consultants often find their work
   A. unstructured.
   B. requiring a high degree of expertise.
   C. isolating.
   D. all of the above.
   E. A and B.

5. Internal consultants must provide quality service to
   A. customers.
   B. management.
   C. the public.
   D. prospects.

6. *Candor is what the job of the internal consultant is all about* means the consultant must
   A. recognize and express organizational realities.
   B. avoid *rocking the boat.*
   C. speak honestly about sensitive issues.
   D. all of the above.
   E. A and C.

7. To be successful, consultants must primarily
   A. present the truth as they see it.
   B. have credibility.
   C. explain the need for change.
   D. use tact.

OBJECTIVE ASSESSMENT (continued)

8. Once you have established a good relationship with a client, the process of discussing changes will proceed positively.
   A. True
   B. False

9. Being an internal consultant may
   A. build employee resentment.
   B. compromise your position in the company.
   C. require constant flexibility.
   D. all of the above.
   E. A and C.

10. Establishing trust requires having
    A. positive mini-behaviors.
    B. a sensitivity to feelings.
    C. professional expertise.
    D. all of the above.
    E. A and C.

11. The best time to use a consultant's services is
    A. during strategic planning.
    B. as damage control.
    C. to make recovery from disaster possible.
    D. just before implementation of a plan.

12. As a consultant, you should beware of
    A. having to do your own data gathering.
    B. complaints going to your boss before they go to you.
    C. being assigned to work with someone who reports to top management only.
    D. all of the above.
    E. B and C.

13. It is easier to
    A. define a problem.
    B. explain symptoms.

14. Which one of the following is not a good interview technique?
    A. restating what the interviewee has said.
    B. giving non-verbal cues.
    C. having an impassive and neutral expression.
    D. setting an agenda.

15. Analyzing the difference between people's optimal and actual competencies is called
    A. Gap Analysis.
    B. Force Field Analysis.
    C. Purpose/People/Product/Process Analysis.

16. Usually, it is better to give
    A. negative rather than positive feedback to clarify the problem.
    B. negative feedback between two positive points.
    C. only positive feedback.

17. During the feedback phase of consulting, you should
    A. keep communicating.
    B. use influence rather than authority.
    C. avoid the sensitive aspects of your research.
    D. all of the above.
    E. A and B.

18. To reach a mutually agreeable solution to a problem, you should first
    A. zero in on the one adjustment that will have the most impact.
    B. focus on the complex causes of the problem.

19. The most essential closure is that you
    A. celebrate your success.
    B. offer your ongoing support.
    C. explain that you would like feedback.
    D. plan your measurement program.

20. Keep the tone of your final discussion
    A. developmental.
    B. judgmental.

21. During implementation
    A. contingency plans should be at the ready.
    B. covert resistance may be taking place.
    C. timely communication is essential.
    D. all of the above.
    E. B and C.

22. Resisters to change should be
    A. circumvented.
    B. brought into the process.
    C. opposed by a majority.
    D. ignored.

OBJECTIVE ASSESSMENT (continued)

23. In marketing your consultant skills, your primary approach should be to
    A. itemize your successes.
    B. anticipate a client's need.
    C. give your credentials.
    D. use the phone not the mail.

24. In packaging your services, it is essential that you have a professionally designed brochure.
    A. True
    B. False

25. If you are called in to solve an immediate problem, you should
    A. focus on it.
    B. be aware of the big picture.
    C. change your employer's expectation.
    D. all of the above.
    E. A and B.

Qualitative Objectives for *The Internal Consultant*

To explain the role of an internal consultant:

Questions 1, 2, 3, 4, 5, 9, 10

To show how to operate as an internal consultant:

Questions 6, 7, 8, 11, 12, 13, 14, 15, 16, 25

To explain closure and implementation:

Questions 18, 19, 20, 21

To discuss dealing with resistance and how to market your services:

Questions 17, 22, 23, 24

ANSWER KEY

1. D	10. D	18. A
2. A	11. A	19. D
3. A	12. E	20. A
4. E	13. B	21. D
5. B	14. C	22. B
6. E	15. A	23. B
7. B	16. B	24. B
8. B	17. E	25. E
9. D		

NOTES

NOTES

NOTES

NOTES

NOTES

NOW AVAILABLE FROM
CRISP PUBLICATIONS

Books • Videos • CD Roms • Computer-Based Training Products

If you enjoyed this book, we have great news for you. There are over 200 books available in the *50-Minute*™ Series. To request a free full-line catalog, contact your local distributor or Crisp Publications, Inc., 1200 Hamilton Court, Menlo Park, CA 94025. Our toll-free number is 800-442-7477.

Subject Areas Include:

Management

Human Resources

Communication Skills

Personal Development

Marketing/Sales

Organizational Development

Customer Service/Quality

Computer Skills

Small Business and Entrepreneurship

Adult Literacy and Learning

Life Planning and Retirement

CRISP WORLDWIDE DISTRIBUTION

English language books are distributed worldwide. Major international distributors include:

ASIA/PACIFIC

Australia/New Zealand: In Learning, PO Box 1051 Springwood QLD, Brisbane, Australia 4127
Telephone: 7-3841-1061, Facsimile: 7-3841-1580   ATTN: Messrs. Gordon

Singapore: Graham Brash (Pvt) Ltd. 32, Gul Drive, Singapore 2262
Telephone: 65-861-1336, Facsimile: 65-861-4815   ATTN: Mr. Campbell

CANADA

Reid Publishing, Ltd., Box 69559-109 Thomas Street, Oakville, Ontario Canada L6J 7R4.
Telephone: (905) 842-4428, Facsimile: (905) 842-9327   ATTN: Mr. Reid

Trade Book Stores: Raincoast Books, 8680 Cambie Street, Vancouver, British Columbia, Canada V6P 6M9.
Telephone: (604) 323–7100, Facsimile: 604-323-2600   ATTN: Ms. Laidley

EUROPEAN UNION

England: Flex Training, Ltd. 9-15 Hitchin Street, Baldock, Hertfordshire, SG7 6A, England
Telephone: 1-462-896000, Facsimile: 1-462-892417   ATTN: Mr. Willetts

INDIA

Multi-Media HRD, Pvt., Ltd., National House, Tulloch Road, Appolo Bunder, Bombay, India 400-039
Telephone: 91-22-204-2281, Facsimile: 91-22-283-6478   ATTN: Messrs. Aggarwal

MIDDLE EAST

United Arab Emirates: Al-Mutanabbi Bookshop, PO Box 71946, Abu Dhabi
Telephone: 971-2-321-519, Facsimile: 971-2-317-706   ATTN: Mr. Salabbai

SOUTH AMERICA

Mexico: Grupo Editorial Iberoamerica, Serapio Rendon #125, Col. San Rafael, 06470 Mexico, D.F.
Telephone: 525-705-0585, Facsimile: 525-535-2009   ATTN: Señor Grepe

SOUTH AFRICA

Alternative Books, Unit A3 Sanlam Micro Industrial Park, Hammer Avenue STRYDOM Park, Randburg, 2194 South Africa
Telephone: 2711 792 7730, Facsimile: 2711 792 7787   ATTN: Mr. de Haas